At Home with Science

Dig and Sow!

How do plants grow?

Written by Janice Lobb
Illustrated by Peter Utton and Ann Savage

KING*f*ISHER

KINGFISHER
Kingfisher Publications Plc
New Penderel House
283-288 High Holborn
London WC1V 7HZ

First published by Kingfisher Publications Plc 2000
10 9 8 7 6 5 4 3 2 1

ITR/0100/FR/128MARWA

Created and designed by Snapdragon Publishing Ltd
Copyright © Snapdragon Publishing Ltd 2000

A CIP catalogue record for this book is available
in the British Library.

ISBN 0 7534 0427 3

Printed in Hong Kong

Author Janice Lobb
Illustrators Peter Utton and Ann Savage

For Snapdragon
Editorial Director Jackie Fortey
Art Director Chris Legee

For Kingfisher
Series Editors Camilla Reid and Emma Wild
Series Art Editor Mike Buckley
DTP Co-ordinator Nicky Studdart
Production Caroline Jackson

Contents

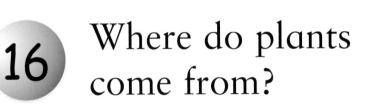
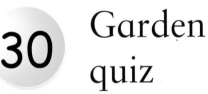
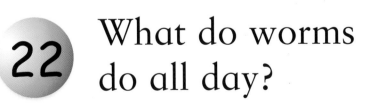

About this book

Have you ever wondered why trees don't fall over, how soil is made or why bees hum? Asking these questions is what being a scientist is all about. This book is about the science that is happening around you, every day, outside in the garden and in your local park. Keep your eyes open and you'll soon be making your own discoveries.

Hall of Fame

Archie and his friends are here to help you. They are each named after famous scientists – apart from Bob the duck, who is a young scientist just like you!

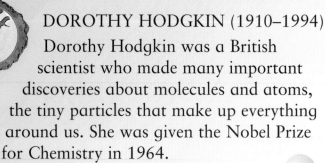

Archie
ARCHIMEDES (287-212BC)
The Greek scientist Archimedes worked out why things float or sink while he was in the bath. According to the story he was so pleased that he leapt out, shouting "Eureka!", which means "I've done it!".

Frank
BENJAMIN FRANKLIN (1706-1790)
This American statesman carried out a famous experiment in 1752. By flying a kite in a storm he showed that a flash of lightning was electricity. He then invented the lightning conductor to protect buildings during storms.

Marie
MARIE CURIE (1867-1934)
Girls did not go to university in Poland, where Marie Curie grew up, so she went to study in Paris, France. She worked on radioactivity and received two Nobel prizes for her discoveries, in 1903 and 1911.

Dot
DOROTHY HODGKIN (1910–1994)
Dorothy Hodgkin was a British scientist who made many important discoveries about molecules and atoms, the tiny particles that make up everything around us. She was given the Nobel Prize for Chemistry in 1964.

See for yourself!

1 Read about the science in your garden, then try the 'See for yourself!' experiments to discover how it works. In science, experiments try to find or show the answers.

2 Carefully read the instructions for each experiment, making sure you follow the numbered instructions in the correct order.

3 Here are some of the things you will need. Have everything ready before you start each experiment.

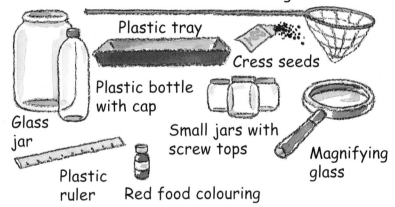

Fishing net

Plastic tray

Cress seeds

Plastic bottle with cap

Glass jar

Small jars with screw tops

Plastic ruler

Red food colouring

Magnifying glass

4 Safety first! ✋

Some scientists take risks to make their discoveries, but our experiments are safe. Just make sure that you tell an adult what you are doing, and get their help when you see the red warning button.

Amazing facts

You'll notice that some words are written in *italics*. You can learn more about them from the glossary at the back of the book. And if you want to find out some amazing facts, look out for the 'Wow!' panels.

WOW!

Look out for the useful tips!

Have fun!

Why is grass green?

Unlike animals, plants make their own food. They do this by absorbing the Sun's *energy* and changing it into food. This process is called *photosynthesis*. In order to do this, plants must contain a substance called *chlorophyll*. Chlorophyll is green in colour, which is why most plants are green.

The food factory

Plants use chlorophyll, *carbon dioxide* and water to make a sugary food called *glucose*. As they do this they release *oxygen* into the air.

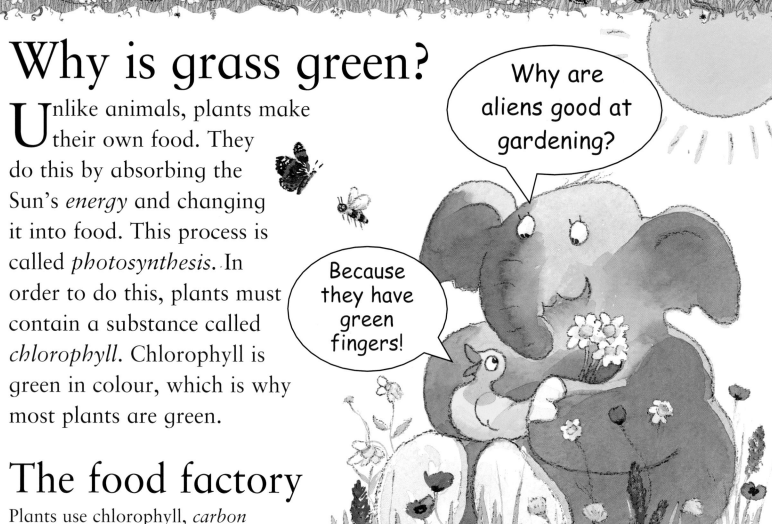

Why are aliens good at gardening?

Because they have green fingers!

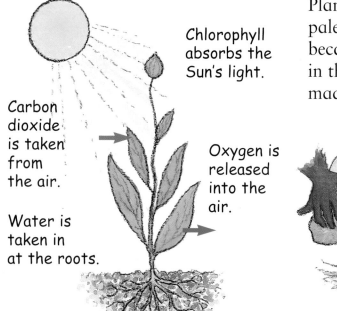

Chlorophyll absorbs the Sun's light.

Carbon dioxide is taken from the air.

Oxygen is released into the air.

Water is taken in at the roots.

Plants under stones are pale and straggly. This is because they are growing in the dark and have not made any chlorophyll.

Archie can't make his own food and must eat plants to live. So, indirectly, his food comes from the Sun too.

6

Fresh air

Too much carbon dioxide in the air can suffocate animals, but plants love it. The oxygen in the air is produced by plants during photosynthesis. Without plants we would not be able to breathe at all. Trees in the world's forests, grass on the plains and *algae* in the sea, all help to keep the air fresh.

WOW!

See for yourself!

1 Watch photosynthesis happening for yourself. Collect some leaves, like privet, bay or geranium. New, fresh ones will work best.

2 Pour some water into a shallow bowl or plastic container and put in the leaves with their undersides facing upwards. To compare them, float one or two leaves the right way up.

3 Leave them in the sunshine for a little while. Then look at them through a magnifying glass. You will see little bubbles of oxygen.

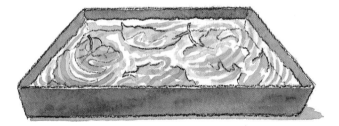

We all need to eat green plants to stay healthy!

Why don't trees fall over?

Why is an elephant like a tree?

Because they both have trunks!

Like most plants, trees need to grow upwards to get as much light as possible. To stop them from falling over, plants have *roots* which spread out under the ground and support them as they grow. As well as supporting a plant, the roots also suck up water from the earth. Trees need thick, woody roots to support their heavy trunks, but smaller plants have thinner roots.

A tree can grow tall because its stem is a firm trunk made of wood. Smaller flowering plants do not make wood. They need water in their stems to stop them from drooping.

Every year a new layer of wood is added on the outside of a tree's trunk, under the bark.

A tree

Woody trunk

Woody roots

By counting the growth rings on a tree-trunk you can tell how old it is.

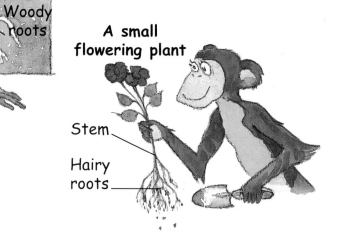

A small flowering plant

Stem

Hairy roots

8

See for yourself!

1 Place a dandelion, a rose, a stick of celery and some twigs into a jar of water. Then put identical plants in another jar without water.

2 Leave both jars for a couple of days, looking at them from time to time. What happens to the plants?

Without water

3 Even without water, woody stems stay stiff, but their flowers and leaves droop and shrivel.

Rose

With water

Without water

4 The stem of the dandelion is supported by the pressure of the water inside it. So, in a jar of water it stands up well, but left out of water it will droop and die within a few hours.

Dandelion

With water

Without water

Big trunks

WOW!

In Africa, there is a tree called the baobab which has an unusual trunk. During the rainy season, the tree stores water inside the trunk, which swells up like a barrel. In dry weather, it uses this water to survive, and the trunk shrinks again.

Don't wait until you see your plants drooping before you water them.

9

What is soil?

Y ou know what soil is – it's the dark, crumbly stuff that you see when you are digging in the garden. But do you know what soil is made of? In fact, it is a mixture of lots of things – small pieces of rock, *minerals*, air and water, plus the remains of dead plants and animals, which we call *humus*. All these different things are found in the layers that make up soil.

See for yourself!

1 Put a handful of soil into a jar. Top it up with water and put the lid on tightly. Now shake up the jar and leave it to stand for a few minutes.

2 The soil will separate into several layers, with the heaviest stones at the bottom and the lighter material, like leaves and twigs, floating at the top.

How is soil made?

Soil starts to form on the surface of bare rocks. Over time, the weather wears away the surface of the rock, flaking off small rock *particles*. These particles collect in cracks and crevices in the rock.

Small plants, such as *moss*, start to grow on top of the fragments of rock. When they die, they are added to the newly formed soil. This humus helps to hold the soil together.

Gradually the soil gets thicker and minibeasts make it their home. Earthworms help to mix up the rock particles and humus. They also let in the air that plant roots need to grow.

Rock particles collect in cracks in the rock.

Small plants start to grow.

Worms help to mix the new soil.

WOW!

Sliding soil

Soil takes a long time to form, but it can be lost very quickly. When people cut down too many trees, the soil becomes loose and the wind can blow it away. It could also be washed away by the rain in a landslide. This is called *erosion*.

Remember to wash the soil off your hands when you have finished.

Do plants eat and drink?

Although plants don't eat and drink like us, they do need food and water to survive. As we have discovered, they make their food from the sunshine and air. They drink by sucking up water from the soil through their long, widely spread roots. The roots also take in minerals, such as magnesium, which keep the plant healthy.

What do plants like to drink?

Root beer!

Keeping healthy

If there is not enough magnesium or iron in the soil, plants can't make enough green chlorophyll and they go yellow or white.

Gardeners use fertilizers, such as manure, to feed plants if the soil does not have enough minerals.

Sickly plant

Healthy plant

Manure

See for yourself!

1 Fill a glass with water and add a few drops of red food colouring. Cut the bottom off a stick of celery and place it in the glass.

2 Leave it for about an hour and then take a look. You will see that the pink colour has crept upwards, carried by the water in the celery stalk.

3 Cut through the celery stalk and you will see the tubes that carry water and sap. Have they changed colour?

4 You can try this with a white flower, like a carnation. If you leave it in the coloured water long enough, the petals will turn pink too.

WOW! Trapped!

The Venus flytrap plant grows in boggy soils which do not provide it with all the minerals it needs. The flytrap has developed an unusual way of adding to its diet - it waits for flies to land on its leaves, then snaps them shut and digests the fly.

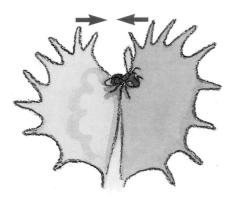

The leaves snap shut and trap the fly.

Cut flowers need to be put in water to stay fresh.

What are flowers for?

Flowers look pretty in the garden, but they also have a useful job to do. They contain the parts of the plant which make *seeds*. These seeds will grow into new plants. Most flowering plants need help with making their seeds. Some use insects to carry their *pollen* from one flower to another. The bright colours and scents of flowers encourage bees and other insects to visit them. Other plants, like grasses, use the wind to carry pollen.

Why is a flower like the letter A?

Because a B comes after it!

How a seed is made

As it searches for *nectar*, the bee rubs against the *stamens*, the male parts of the flower, and picks up fine yellow pollen grains.

Flying on to the next flower, the bee rubs against the *carpels*, the female parts of the plant, leaving the pollen behind.

The grains of pollen stick to the carpels and then grow down to join with tiny egg cells inside. These will soon become seeds.

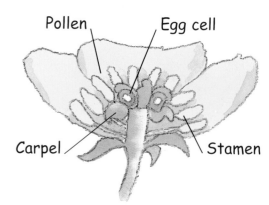

Pollen

Egg cell

Carpel

Stamen

See for yourself! ✋

1 Look at a flower bud. Around the outside are green *sepals*, which protect the flower when it is growing.

Sepal

Sepal

2 Now look at a flower. The bright *petals*, which may be white or coloured, attract insects to the flower.

Petal

3 Inside the flower are the stamens sticking up from its centre. Try shaking them onto dark paper to see if they leave a yellow dust.

Stamen

4 Find a flower which is losing its petals and cut it in half. (Ask an adult to help you with this.) Can you see all the different parts the plant uses to make a seed?

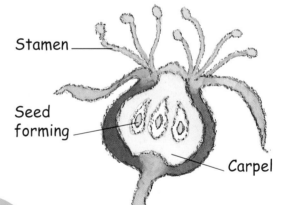

Stamen

Seed forming

Carpel

Fruity packages

WOW!

The fruit is the part of the plant which carries and protects the seeds. Fruits can be juicy, like tomatoes and peppers, or dry, like poppy capsules. Each pip that is packed inside a tomato is a tiny seed.

Seed

To keep a rose in flower, take off the dead flower heads.

Where do plants come from?

Every country has its own plants which grow there naturally. We call these *native* plants. You may find some of them in the countryside or in a wildflower garden. If they grow where we don't want them, we call them *weeds*. Most gardens contain *introduced plants*, which people have collected from somewhere else. When explorers went to new countries, they brought plants back with them. When people settled in new places, they often took plants with them. So gardens contain a mixture of plants from many countries.

What did one plant say to the other plant?

Have we been introduced?

How plants spread

When a plant is growing well in one place, it flowers and makes seeds. These help the plant spread to new places.

Other seeds are eaten by animals and birds, and pass through their bodies.

Some seeds are carried away from the parent plant by the wind or rain.

See for yourself!

1 Pick a dandelion 'clock' and blow the seeds. See how far they go before they reach the ground. The little fluffy parachute at the top of each seed helps it to float in air.

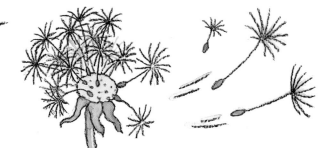

2 Look out for tiny seeds and other seeds with parachutes or wings. Are they shot through the air, or do they 'fly' or spin?

Seeds with wings

3 Look for seeds that hook on to animal fur, or your clothes. Can you find larger seeds that roll away from the plants?

4 Look out for seeds in mud on your shoes or on the wheels of your bicycle.

WOW!

Seeds ahoy!

Coconut palms grow along sandy beaches on tropical islands. The coconuts are their seeds. If a coconut falls into the sea, it can float many kilometres to another island, where it may *germinate* and grow.

Never touch berries you don't know—they may be poisonous!

What did the frost say to the seed?

Don't shoot!

How do seeds grow?

Every seed has the beginnings of a new plant inside it, waiting to grow. This is called an *embryo*. In the springtime, when there is plenty of sun and rain, the seed starts to grow. Using the special food stored inside the seed, a little *shoot* grows up towards the sunlight, whilst a root grows downwards, looking for water. When a seed starts to grow, we say it germinates.

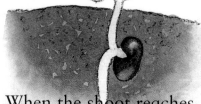

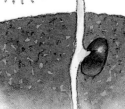

Plants grow towards the Sun.

Shoot

Seed

Even if you plant a seed upside down, the shoot will grow upwards and the roots downwards.

Roots

The shoot grows quickly, feeding on the food stored inside its seed.

When the shoot reaches the light, it starts to make its own food from the Sun.

See for yourself!

1 Line the base of a dish with a paper towel. Wet it with warm water and sprinkle some cress seeds on it.

2 Find a box big enough to hold the dish. Cut a window in the lower half of one end. Put the dish inside and close the lid.

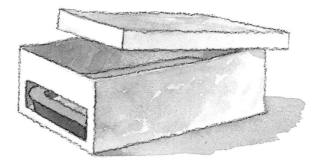

3 Put the box in a warm, light place and keep the seeds moist with water.

4 Do the cress plants grow straight upwards or do they grow towards the sunlight, coming into the side of the box?

WOW!

Running plants

Some plants produce baby plants instead of seeds. Strawberry plants and spider plants put out *runners*. These are long stems which stretch along the ground. At the end of each stem is a miniature plant complete with leaves and roots. This will grow in soil if you plant it in a pot.

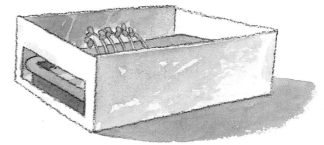

Try growing a plant from an apple or avocado seed.

19

Do plants die in winter?

Winter is a hard time for plants. There is not enough sunshine to give them energy. They can't get enough water from frozen soil. Winds batter them and they may break under the weight of snow. So *deciduous* plants store food in the summer, then shed their leaves in the autumn. Small plants may die back to ground level. The parts of the plant that are left bare or underground rest through the winter. Plants that die after they flower leave seeds to grow into new plants.

What has eyes but cannot see?

A potato!

Storing food

The stored food in seeds is used when they start to grow, or germinate.

Roots

The bases of leaves and stems called bulbs store food under the ground. Plants use bulbs to grow again in the spring.

Bulb

Many plants, such as carrots, store food in their roots, ready to grow again in the spring.

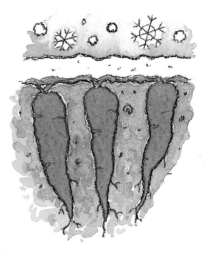

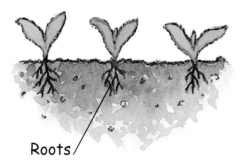

See for yourself!

1 Pick twigs in winter or early spring. You can see the buds which will grow into new leaves and flowers. Some, like horse chestnuts, have sticky buds.

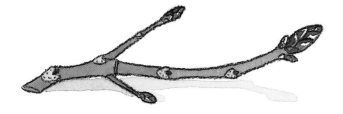

2 Put them in water and watch them open and grow. You will find the tree was not as dead as it looked.

3 Look in your vegetable rack. Each 'eye' on a potato, each clove of a garlic, is a bud waiting to grow into a new plant.

4 Try leaving vegetables in a dark cupboard for a couple of weeks. They will start to sprout and shoots will begin to grow.

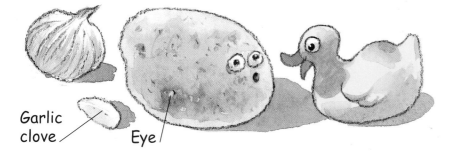

Garlic clove

Eye

Desert flowers

WOW!

There are plants that make seeds so that they can live through very hot, dry weather. These seeds can lie for years in desert soil. Then, when rain comes, they germinate and flower, bringing colour to the desert landscape.

Soak a bean and open it to see the baby plant inside!

What do worms do all day?

Earthworms may not look like busy creatures, but in fact they are very hard working. Worms feed by swallowing soil as they burrow. At night, they come to the surface and pull dead plants down under the ground. All this activity is very good for the soil and for the plants living in it. It helps to get rid of dead plants and to bring air to the roots of the living ones.

How can you tell where a worm's head is?

Tickle its tummy and see which end laughs!

Woodlouse

Worm cast

Leaf being pulled down

Worm burrow

Mouth

Bristles

Segment

An earthworm wriggles along by changing the shapes of its body segments.

The worm stretches out parts of its body

and then pulls along the rest.

See for yourself!

1 To make a wormery, find a large jar (like a pickle jar). Place a plastic bottle inside it with a lid on it. (Leave the bottle out if the jar is quite small.)

2 Fill the jar (but not the bottle) with layers of sand, soil and compost, then finish off with some dead leaves. Cover the sides of the jar with dark paper.

3 Collect three or four earthworms and put them in the top. Stretch a layer of netting across the mouth of the jar and secure with an elastic band.

4 Put the jar in a cool cupboard, making sure that the soil is kept damp, but not soggy. After a few days, check to see what has happened to the soil.

Worm burrows

You should find that the worms have mixed the layers of sand and soil.

Giant worms!

WOW!

One of the world's largest earthworms lives in a tropical river valley in the Australian state of Victoria. The Great Gippsland earthworm can grow to over 3.5 metres long, and makes a gurgling sound as it munches its way through the soil. Giant earthworms are rare, so there are laws to protect them.

Set your worms free when you have finished with them.

Why do bees hum?

Why does a bee hum?

Because it has forgotten the words!

Bees and many other insects hum or buzz. They make the noise with their wings when they fly. Although insect wings look delicate, they are quite stiff. When the wings flap downwards, the air under them is pushed out of the way in little puffs. This lifts the insect up into the air. When the wings flap up, the air above them is moved away. The way the wings move makes the air *vibrate*. When these little puffs of air reach our ears, we hear them as sound.

See for yourself!

1 You can make the air vibrate. Take a piece of thin plastic, like a ruler or a phone card, and wave it to and fro quickly near your face. Can you feel the air moving in little puffs?

2 Then put the ruler on the table so that about three-quarters of it sticks out beyond the table edge. Hold down one edge firmly with one hand. Bend the other end and let it go quickly. Can you hear a sound?

Sizes and sounds

Mosquitoes have little wings that make the air vibrate very fast. This action makes a very high, whining sound.

Mosquito

Mosquito

The bumble-bee's larger wings make the air vibrate more slowly. This makes a low buzzing sound.

Bee

3 Now place the ruler on the table so that only half of it sticks out and repeat. Then a quarter. Listen to the different sounds made by the ruler moving through the air. Like a bee's wings, the ruler makes the air vibrate.

You can't hear the sound made by a butterfly's wings, because they flap too slowly.

Butterfly

WOW!

Musical legs

Not all insects make sounds with their wings. Grasshoppers and crickets chirrup. To do this, they vibrate the air by rubbing their back legs against the edges of their hard *wing cases*.

Remember that bees and wasps can sting - so look but dont touch.

Who visits the garden?

The daily life of every animal is spent in a constant search for food. If there is not enough food where they live, the animals must travel to find it, and your garden may be the place that they visit. Sit quietly in the corner of the garden and watch the visitors as they come and go. They may fly in, they may come up from the ground or they may run in from under a fence or hedge. Some will be more welcome than others!

> Why wasn't the butterfly invited to the dance?

> Because it was a moth ball!

Keep a look out

Butterflies and bees are attracted to the scent and colour of flowers. They eat the flowers' nectar.

Buddleia

Aphid

Ladybird

Ladybirds are good insects to have around. They eat the aphids that feed on many garden plants and damage them.

Woodpeckers search for ants and other insects on the lawn. Other birds, like pigeons, look for seeds and snails.

Pigeon

Woodpecker

See for yourself!

1 In winter, when food is scarce, you can help your local wildlife by putting out food for them. A range of food will attract a variety of creatures. Avoid giving birds bread as this is not very good for them.

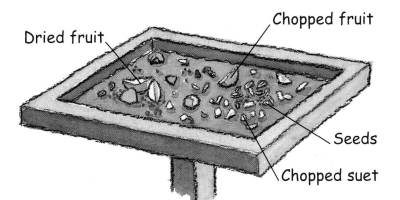

Dried fruit

Chopped fruit

Seeds

Chopped suet

Make sure that you also leave out water.

Tits and sparrows enjoy a coconut.

Birds may not be the only visitors to your table – squirrels love nuts too.

2 Make a note of what animals you see and how often they return to the garden.

WOW!

Night-time visitors

Many of your garden's guests come and go while you are asleep. Foxes and hedgehogs are common night-time visitors and, if you live in the country, you may get deer, rabbits or badgers. Look out for the tracks and droppings they leave behind.

Make a conservation corner in your garden for wildlife to visit.

27

What lives in the pond?

A pond is the *habitat* for all kinds of different plants and animals. This means that the pond gives them food, water and shelter – all the things they need to survive. Some plants live at the bottom of the pond. Others float on the surface or live on the banks. The plants make oxygen which keeps the water fresh for the animals that live there. Small animals such as pond snails feed on the plants, and frogs lay their *frogspawn* in them. The frogspawn hatches into tadpoles which turn into frogs.

Where do fish sleep?

In water beds!

Baby tadpoles nibble weed.

Frogspawn

Toadspawn

Older tadpoles feed on tiny animals.

See for yourself! ✋

1 With an adult's help, collect some pond water. Then fish out some pondweed using a net. Be very careful not to fall in!

2 Put some of the pond water in a deep white bowl. Using a magnifying glass, look closely at what is floating and swimming around in the water.

Mosquito larva

Algae

Water flea

3 Now add the pondweed to your bowl. What minibeasts are hiding in it?

Pond snail

Weed

4 Sit quietly by the pond to see what other insects you can spot. Where are they? How do they move about?

Dragonfly

Whirligig beetle

Water boatman

Walking on water!

Some insects, such as pond-skaters, are able to glide quickly over the surface of still water. Their long legs are stopped from breaking through because of *surface tension*. This makes the water behave like an elastic skin.

WOW!

Be sure to return your minibeasts to the pond!

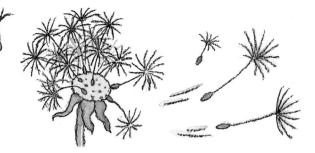

Garden quiz

1 What is the green colour in leaves called?

a) Iron
b) Chlorophyll
c) Carbon dioxide

2 How can you find out how old a tree is?

a) By counting its roots
b) By counting its branches
c) By counting the rings in its trunk

3 Where can you find a layer of humus?

a) In the soil
b) In the air
c) In leaves

4 What does a plant called a Venus fly trap eat?

a) Nectar
b) Insects
c) Frogs

5 What do bees carry from one flower to another?

a) Carpels
b) Pollen
c) Seeds

6 How does a dandelion spread its seeds?

a) It uses the sun
b) It uses the sea
c) It uses the wind

7 What does a seed do when it germinates?

a) It dies back
b) It begins to grow
c) It spreads its seeds

8 How does a bulb help a plant live through the winter?

a) By spreading seeds
b) By losing leaves
c) By storing food

9 What does an earthworm use to pull leaves down into the soil?

a) Its mouth
b) Its tail
c) Its segments

10 Which of these insects walks on water?

a) The pond-skater
b) The bee
c) The butterfly

30

Answers on page 32

Glossary

Algae
Plants which grow in water or on moist ground, with no stems, leaves or flowers.

Carbon dioxide
A gas present in the air and used by green plants to photosynthesize.

Carpels
Female parts of a flower, containing egg-cell.

Chlorophyll
Green pigment in plants that absorbs the energy from the Sun.

Deciduous
Trees or shrubs that lose their leaves in the autumn.

Embryo
Baby plant inside a seed, forming parts which need to grow.

Energy
Gives something the ability to do work. Light and heat are forms of energy.

Erosion
Wearing away of rock and soil by the weather.

Frogspawn
A mass of frog's eggs protected by jelly and laid in water.

Germinate
Begin to grow, sprout a new plant from a seed.

Glucose
Sugary food that green plants make during photosynthesis.

Habitat
The natural home of a plant or animal.

Humus
A substance made from decayed plants, leaves and animal matter.

Introduced plants
Brought into a region from another area by humans.

Minerals
Chemicals which are found naturally in rocks and soil which do not come from living things.

Moss
A variety of small flowerless plant, growing as a thick mass on rocks or tree trunks.

Native
Originating in a particular place or area.

Nectar
Sugary fluid, at the base of many petals, that attracts insects and birds.

Oxygen
A gas in the air essential for animals to breathe, made when green plants photosynthesize.

Particle
Very little parts or small pieces of something.

Petals
Outer parts of a flower, used mainly to attract feeding insects.

Photosynthesis
Process by which green plants make food using energy from the Sun.

Pollen
Tiny grains made in flowers, which contain male sex cells. When they fertilize female egg-cells, seeds are produced.

Root
Underground part of flowering plant or fern.

Runners
Stems growing out flat along the ground, producing baby plantlets at the tips.

Seeds
The part of a plant from which a new plant grows.

Sepals
Outer, green parts of the flower bud, which protect petals as they develop.

Shoot
A new plant growth growing out from a seed above ground; a stem with leaves and buds.

Stamens
Male parts of a plant, which produce pollen.

Surface tension
A force in the surface water which makes it behave like an elastic skin.

Vibrate
To move back and forth quickly.

Weed
A wild plant growing among cultivated plants or elsewhere unwanted.

Wing cases
Hardened front wings, not used for flying, but to protect hind wings.

Index

Answers to the Garden quiz on page 30

1 Chlorophyll. **2** By counting the rings in its trunk.
3 In the soil. **4** Insects. **5** Pollen. **6** It uses the wind.
7 It begins to grow. **8** By storing food. **9** Its mouth.
10 The pond-skater.